Vivid Companion

West Virginia University Press, Morgantown 26506

First edition published 2004 by West Virginia University Press
Printed in the United States of America
Third Printing

10 09   9 8 7 6 5 4 3

ISBN 0 937058-82-3 (alk. paper)

Library of Congress Cataloguing-in-Publication Data

McKinney, Irene.
Vivid Companion : Irene McKinney
        p.   cm.

1. Title

IN PROCESS

Library of Congress Control Number: 2004111041

Cover Design: Lisa Bridges Design
Cover photo by Steven Gelberg
Book Design by Than Saffel
Interior typeface: Adobe Jensen Pro
Printed in USA

Vivid Companion

Poems

Irene McKinney

Vandalia Press

A Division of The West Virginia University Press

Morgantown 2004

Before I traveled my road
I was my road.

Antonio Porchia

Acknowledgments

I wish to thank the editors of the following publications, where some of these poems first appeared:

American Voice: "Viridian Days"

Appalachian Heritage: "Dark Rain"

Appalachian Journal: "Woods Burning"

Artful Dodge: "Fodder"

Arts & Letters: "Ravi Sings" and "Adobe"

The Bridge: "The Stutter"

Chattahoochee Review: "Monkey Heart"

Cincinnati Poetry Review: "The Testimony of Harriet Worden"

Clackamas Literary Review: "Constant Companion"

Confluence: "Filthy Weather"

Georgia Review: "Face," "At 24," and "Homage to the Baroness Elsa von Freytag Loringhoven"

Kenyon Review: "Fame" and "The Surgery"

Kestrel: "Catherine Baker: Arrival at Oneida Creek, 1848;" "Mary Cragin: The Honeymoon, 1834;" "Professor Mears of Hamilton College Speaks to the Court;" "Sarah Burt: The Doll Burning, 1851;" "The Tree of Life Tapestry: Jessie Kinsley, 1927;" "Full Moon: Sitting Up Late at My Father's Bedside;" "Low Red Moon;" "Three Three Three;" and "Redemption"

Kestrel 10th Anniversary Issue: "Home"

Nightsun: "Handholds"

Poetry Motel: "Hiding"

Poetry Northwest: "The Dream Feast," "Ready," and "Personal"

River Oak Review: "Low Red Moon"

Salmagundi: "Solitude in the Oneida Community: Victor Cragin Noyes, 1866"
Solo: "Gray's Anatomy"
South Dakota Review: "Illuminated Manuscript" and "Ironweed"
Sow's Ear: "Atavistic"
Spillway: "Ironweed"
Washington Square: "Our Lady of the Iguanas"

Great River Arts Institute and the letterpress publisher Golgonooza Press published "The Walk" in a portfolio of broadsides.

"Viridian Days" was reprinted in *Her Words: Critical Essays And Conversations On Appalachian Women's Poetry*, Felicia Mitchell, editor (University of Tennessee Press, 2002), and also in *Wild Sweet Notes: Fifty Years Of West Virginia Poetry*, edited by Barbara Smith and Kirk Judd (Publisher's Place, 2000).

"Fodder" and "Viridian Days" were reprinted in *Backcountry: Contemporary Writing In West Virginia*, Irene McKinney, editor (Vandalia Press, West Virginia University, 2002).

I would like to thank the Virginia Center for the Creative Arts, the MacDowell Colony, and the West Virginia Commission for the Arts for grants and fellowships which gave me time to write.

I am very grateful to Maggie Anderson, Jan Beatty, Devon McNamara, and Aaron Smith for reading this manuscript, and for their support of the poems.

Contents

III.

IV.

V.

I

Our Lady Of The Iguanas

After a photograph by Graciela Iturbide

I've taken the powers of darkness and put them on my head.
Some of the iguanas lean far over my shoulder and stare
at passersby, others strain their necks upward toward
God knows what. Below the scales and claws and beady eyes,
my face is rapt. This headdress is wider than the path

I walk on and you'd better clear the way. If I look down
abruptly they will fall and crash apart, but for now
they glare at everything while I convey them to you.
The dress I wear is scattered with flying mariposas on
a black background. The ground is all. I walk upon the ground;

my head is otherwise. God knows these reptile faces as
his own, mine too. My eyes become all pupils, black as blackest
shining hair. As his iguanas ride my head to market,
I advertise his works and make my own. Their jointed arms
and splayed-out feet that clutch my scalp, their rigid

reptile smiles, their stench. When have they ever been
so elevated? And when have I? In Juchitan the women
carry them into the busy world, braving the scaly
ones so close the brain, the bold exposure in the marketplace,
the proud display in broad daylight of what crawls out

3

of the dark. There are seven of them, seven carved heads
looking every which way, posturing and rising.

— ▬ —

And if I say that I admire her stance, you might ask
what I mean. I mean she carries what she can never understand.
She carries what we are repulsed by, she carries
the grimace, the rictus smile of the iguana.
I mean she carries me away, she stares through clouds and

becomes cloudy and I follow her gaze which goes upwards
and stays bemused in spite of all that bears down on her.
Some are cold, one is murderous, others are oblivious,
some crouch down. Our reptile mind pulsates beneath
the reptile bodies. They are our kin, and alien to the bone.

The Komodo, the copperhead. They shine. We think we could
escape but we don't, we think we have the means to crush them
but we don't. We come as close as we can, and then pull back
and try again. A girl in my class once began to scream when
I read a story with a blacksnake in it. "I can't stand it,"

she told us, "It's always been this way, you have to understand."
We did, and so I stopped reading, hoping that tomorrow she would
have more strength to listen. Her thin hands fluttered about
her face and her eyes were wild with fear. She stood, and sat,
and stood again, about to run. I want her to see this photograph,

to see how one may lift and carry pounds of icy flesh and bone.

———

I want to lift and carry all this icy flesh and bone.
I want to walk out into the public square with the unknown
on my head and not blink or shuffle. I want to have a gaze
as translucent as water or the shine from scales. To don
the headdress for the ritual, to bear it through the ceremony

and no longer, because I know it must be temporary,
the weight unwieldy, the effect bizarre. And the people
around me will nod and look away, and look back again
at something so familiar that they think they're dreaming
and then they know they're not. The piles of vegetables

around me glow in reds and greens, the peppers fat
with flesh and sheen, the apples shining in their reddish
skins, the onions and garlic sending out signals of smell,
the heraldic meats hanging in display, the sepia barley,
wheat, the grains of corn in heaps, and through them,
among them, Our Lady walks the dusty aisles.

Gray's Anatomy

This is terrifying. The thin overleaf
And then the marbeled blue
The red striation

The face stripped   the breasts
Veined and brilliant

The sacramental pose   this is my body
I present its blood and meat

The eyes starting from the head
The formal dance step forward

Burning, flayed. Even the sex.
Nothing is saved.

They step off the page and wander the earth.
This is not our fault.

The Surgery

While I lay on the table in darkness,
they opened my side, removed my guts,
and placed them on a dampened sponge
beside me. But too soon
I started to awake, knowing the life
was very small inside me, rising
in a round drop of consciousness
and grieving for my body
which I still knew so well.
I wasn't sad for myself, but
as for a friend I was losing.

And then my eyes fluttered open
for a second and there above me
leaned the face of the nurse,
Dora. She said "Oh my goodness"
softly, and without alarm, and
cradled my head in her arms
while they closed me up
and I cried a little for the body
which was coming back,
the home of all grief.

The Stutter

I wait while he tries to finish,
the stutter rolling around and around on
a bearing; you would have to value your
speech enormously to wait like that
for it to show itself. It makes me want
to whine and cry out like a dog, it makes
me twist and shudder for the word
that will not fall into place, that flutters
on the end of the tongue forever.

How can I go on waiting? Can I
get up and go? Can I ask to come back
later, after it's come out?
Finally, I want to ask him to
write it down. But I've set myself
here as a listener, I bow my head
toward him, and it's not that this is
so different from everything else, but
I need to forget about time. In the interval,
in all the spaces, I can think
what I would say if I were him.

False sympathy, I'd say, you don't
know anything. Later, I read his books.
They are elegant, graceful, musical,
precise. He is speaking and speaking,
pouring toward his listeners. When he

comes down to dinner he doesn't try
to say hello, not sure that it will happen.
He smiles instead. The forms of the world
are dead set against him, but there's
a continuous voice in his head
and it goes on speaking.

Clitoral

after Hardy

They sing their aching song –
all of us do – yes,
the blond, the tall, the willowy,
  and some of us swear and sing;
I shine the flashlight in each face....
  Ah God, we're getting old.
How the grey rain comes down this morning.

They clear their studios –
the young women and the worn ones – yes,
the painters, the sculptors, cleaning the blood
  from their thighs;
and they build a morning-glory bower....
Good Lord, my body hurts;
and a hurricane blows up from the Carolinas.

We meet in the dining hall –
men and women – yes,
and among the arbor vitae mazes
  and dark bitter smell of plants,
while the Holsteins graze and moon....
  Lord, my body is lonely.
And the sweet flesh shrinks no matter what I say.

We leave the gathering-place
and go to our chosen homes – all of us go,
back to our couches and kitchen curtains and dogs
    but we go with the clitoris,
beaten, happy, sore, ignored....
    clitoris the nerve of the mind,
and the cold rain sluices down my skin.

Fodder

So I was the Scavenger-Child, whuffling
in filthy attics, scrounging for
broken-backed editions of Edgar Allen Poe
covered with pigeon-droppings, accumulating
old yellowed books from abandoned schoolhouses

buried in the woods, smelling of piss
and mire and all abuzz with giant wasps
building a nest in the pump organ.
These were my fabulous loves, my secret
foods. There were my handholds

into shaky light, my emergence from
the pit, and loving the furniture of
the pit, my dedication to the darkness
and the shadows of fireflies' bodies
found between the smelly pages, the vile

effluvium of bookworms' paths trekking
with intention through one after the other,
out one cover into the next, eating
their way through shelf after shelf,
Byron, *Sheep Shearing in America*,

Kiss me Deadly to *Paradise Lost*, and
Lo! The Bird. Why should a hungry worm
care what it ate? It was all paper
and words, all black magic marks
in an unmarked world, all height and

depth and beautiful fodder, a method
of moving the eyes until they brimmed
with startlement, the swollen pupils
reading themselves to death, and up
beside it, and into it.

Ravi Sings

The water-glug sounds of the tabla;
the dark dervish, the white cotton.
Past the glistening windows, one by
one by one; he opens his throat
all the way and calls for God,
longing and reconciliation seared together,
the great cry rising up out of
the open throat; O the deepest
nerve pressed upon; O the
clitoral pain, moving falsetto
up by stages over the drone
of the hum of the world and
the planets, the moon, the
plane of the ghosts and demons,
pulling harder against the gravity
of this life; the voice a great
book full of knowing that
longing goes on and on;
a gagging, a shaking of the
glottal, a shadow-voice beside it,
healing as it burns the open throat,
the esraj crying in its strings,
the ululation straining up
from the drone. I stare into
the turning tape and the sweet
powerful shadows come into
my ear; that someone could cry

for God in such a way; that
I could cry with him. Seethala
Lakshmi. Six and three-fourths beats.

Fame

That I would become known;
that someone would know me.
I would be recognized, and not
pitiable; and I would remain
as strong as I was, if not stronger,
and overcome my circumstances
through sheer will, and that
others younger or less talented
would not become known,
or at least not until I was.
Then, that recognition would
reward me for all I'd undergone,
my bravery of thought, my refusal
of dishonest love, and my goodwill
would be returned to me manyfold,
after the years and years.
And I would not be bitter, nor petty,
nor would I act on selfish interests,
nor suppress my generosity.
And none of this was me.

Ironweed

Everything resists; there is iron in the roots
and the squared-off stem, silted into its deepest chambers,

and this weed stands on the slope above the dry creekbed
and refuses nearly everything. It refuses a large and showy

flower; it tried that in another life, when it was an orchid.
It refuses to be pulled out of the ground without shrieking

like a mandrake, and it refuses to let those drops
of Mary's blood ooze from its stem. In the locust tree

above it, an army of cicadas is drilling holes
in the afternoon. Each of them hoists up a pneumatic drill

between its knees. The females have an ovipositor
like a curved iron thorn; they jackhammer their eggs

into the hide of the tree. Later the damaged branches
will fall off, but they don't care. Whatever lasts

resists until it can't. Do you know what I mean?
To someone trying to grow a life, our world casts

itself in a thick iron bark. She hones herself
almost beyond belief. Exhaustion is her flower.

Personal

None of this is personal, not the way you'd think.
The moon keeps on traveling and I can see it
from my balcony each night and each night
different but it's not my own, not like we want

things to be our very own. But it sways me
nevertheless and stands in for certain losses
and gains and for even that much I'm grateful.
I stand at the back door and stare.

Constant Companion

Two days enclosed by rain, hugged up
in this room with no amusement but my voice.
So now it's time to take off all my clothes
and dance around alone; the belly scars, the
pads of flesh okay, and okay the slippery breasts
with their soft surprised pink seals, and equally
okay the body hair, the freckles, darkenings
that flesh is bound for, the overlap and burn.
Here in this rainy box, I've left it all outside,
the crowded kitchen and the laundry tub,
the judging looks. Except the birds:
in their variety out there they peep and croon,
and there's an orchestra of black crickets.
This voice is my constant companion, looking
at the morning glories draped on a lovely thing
of lathe and wire, a frame for burgeoning,
cascading down in blue. You say it's not
okay? You say it's unlovely, even ugly
the way the feet splay out, the way age
grabs you by the face? Okay. I'm dancing
to the Mahotella Queens and singing along
with their male groaners Ah Way, Ah Way!
That's the kind of thing I do in here, where
it gets as dark as you can get at night and
the air is saturated with rain and fog, and
the voice, the bud of the voice, has a chance.

II

Mary Cragin: The Honeymoon, 1834

There was a perfumed balm
my mother brought from France
I used to put between my legs,

and on the marks of the stays.
When I met George I was wearing it,
and my favorite garnet pin.

Oh Lord my God, don't ask me to forgo
my thighs, my scent, my purple gem, and make me
worthy to receive. Nonetheless,

He didn't see fit to at that time and
George began to put his hands on me, and press
my sides. I gave and gave.

And we abused ourselves: the marriage of
the bodies went on and on. I wanted to see
the light, and later when Brother Noyes began

to speak I saw it. Light broke in the stale
kitchen, again and again,
and went away. I want the light

that prevails. Look at the Living Waters
in him, how they stream to me.
Why is the truth not in us?

We will wear it out, strain forward
to where I can see. No Half-way.
None of us can do it alone. Congress,

the bridge from one to the other.

Catherine Baker:
Arrival At Oneida Creek, 1848

Smell of hot wood in the Burnside stove,
smell of baked potatoes, smell of cornbread and molasses.
All that winter we worked in the cabin, three families.
The men came in from the snow, and the air swirled
in our skirts. Beans, then. Strong coffee.
And Mary, crying. Two rooms, and so
we wrapped together. Raw wind,
that drove us toward a foody center.
Biscuits. Hand-shelling corn.
Hand-grown, hand-worked, the handy men.
It was hard but I was in a warm place.
The warmest I have known.

The Testimony Of Harriet Worden, 1850

When I was twelve, my Community father asked me what I knew:
he said my body needed to be taught its clearest ways, and for
that purpose he consulted with a mother to seek out the one
most fitted to open me to myself. Mr. Cragin is a kindly man,
whose trials and strengths are known to all here. He taught me
to keep accounts at the Trap Works, and I loved him well.

Mrs. Cragin came to see me in my room, and we had tea and cakes.
She told me frankly he would know the deepest motion
need not hurt, and he would stay with me until
my pleasure came around. In this way, I would be introduced
in Ascending Fellowship, entered by what he knew from his travails,
while he touched in me my youth. This satisfied me pretty much,

since the older girls had told me of their times, and the preparation
for the feast. After consulting Father Noyes, all of us
agreed on an evening after supper when I would visit his rooms.
He was my father too. Do you see? I needn't crave after my father
all my life, and break my mind and body on him, for since all men
here are my fathers, I will never suffer that deprivation. He was my father

and he opened me. My natural father worked with him for twenty years,
and trusted him. They told me I needn't fear conception, since
they'd practiced the Continence and control for all that time. I was
to open and learn, and that is what I did. He read me, first,
The Song of Solomon: " His left hand is under my head, and his right
hand doth embrace me." He undid my waist, and nourished himself:

"The fig tree putteth forth her green figs, and the vines with the
tender grape give a good smell." Such a fragrance! As though
the hay were sweetly piled, the fruits gathered, come ripe and full,
the flowers in our gardens heaped, pile on pile at once! I suckled,
he did too, he fed me well, and made a sound

                          as calves do at their mothers.
Once I shuddered at my tenderness, and then he stopped
                                and gave me lemonade.

He had some too and smiled at me, his eyes alight. "Little Sister,
I have this now for you, hold me and pass it on," he said,
and eased me down. After some hours I cried, and leaned
my head against his breast. "Bless you," he said. "Remember,
you are as true as any man. Use this well." And I left,
and was never with him in that way again.

Sarah Burt: The Doll Burning, 1851

Mine was wearing a voile frock
with satin edging. She was in
the way. Each day I squeezed her
and dressed her, till her little features
felt like mine. I wanted her,
like a candy, her shiny apple lips,
the ping of her porcelain face I flicked
with my nails. Our teacher asked us
what we felt when we held them.

I lift its easy legs, I bend its arms.
It sits where I fold it, its white
clear cheeks centered with fever-spots.
Of course it's sick, I tend it by bending
it to my strength, if it aches it doesn't know.
I would never wear such stupid lace.

She asks us to sit in a circle
around the stove, holding the throbbing bodies
in our laps, and to speak out now,
and hold them up before the light.

These fruity cheeks are not the ones
we pick from the living tree, working
together. Sugar-tit toes that can't
be sucked. Navel into a sawdust belly.

A mother from the Children's House brings in
a little baby. It smells of milk
and doesn't want to be handled around
the circle. It's cutting teeth, chews
on its bib, and makes a run of sounds
so full of running water
we all laugh.

And now we stand and
sing: we each pass by
the open stove, and toss our sawdust in.

Solitude In The Oneida Community:
Victor Cragin Noyes, 1866

My Father's house has many mansions and none
of them for me. Half-dark, in oaks behind the house
I heard the solitary owl and knew it knew my name.

How can I be victor over the busy lives that cluster
around me like naked bees? I walked below the hives
and shook with the interminable hum of many, blister

of sweetness, incessant buzz. So many, lifting up
the honey-grains, gathering pollen in the hollyhocks.
I shudder at so much life, the lines of flight

twining around me. There is no room to think in.
House and grounds are bright with leaves this morning,
and the troupe of strawberry-pickers sing in the field,

but I, I want to hear my name called singly, and alone
to know what ails me, and to crush against it.
In the Children's House my very mother Mary

held me with the others, and beside me was the shadow
of Victoria, my twin, dead in infancy while
I went on, my right side cut away from my left,

my missing half gone off into the barn-owl's rustle,
into the blue open faces of the chicory and asters
waiting along the footpath where I stare out of my self

to find her, wanting Him to know I am still upright.
It is too bright here! Perhaps there is a time for the heart
to open, but not now: now is a time for clenching tight

and facing down the inner dark of the room where He
sent me. I was afraid, afraid, – already I have lost
so much, I was born beside it. I was told to touch her,

make my self slide in where she was, smelling of milk
and laundry, – and at the last gasp I was removed
from the body of my loss, and spiraled down into the shade

and dank breath of my mother drowned, and Victoria
holding out her final arms. How can I share with them
what is unborn? I'm cold. This quilt of lives

can't warm me. Here's a dropped bobbin, spooling away,
spun down the icy ruts in frozen mud of the road.
There is no victory in my name, – I pluck apart

its skein, the red joining. In the streets of Utica
a skirl of snow, dream-patches shifting: and these,
these people of the world, such a scald

of burning voices, clamor of market, bodies moving
like streaks of fire, – O galvanized, mire
of the morning on Bleeker, torn threads unwoven.

Professor Mears Of Hamilton College Speaks To The Court

Ladies and Gentleman of the county, I am appalled to sit
in the same air with these young women. We asked for the truth,

and now I am afraid we have it. *She sits so straight* Such filth,
such lewdness spews forth from their mouths. *And her eyes*

are so clear The rutting of the coarsest animals is not vile
beside them. I cannot believe the fathers at Oneida

not only countenance such seduction of their daughters,
but they have a hand in planning such abuses! *My hands are sweating,*

and my palms are hot We must dig down deeper, even to
the bottom of this pile of offal. The corruption in

our midst will reach our sons and daughters if we do not
cut it away. *Her breasts are like two does, they strain*

against the printed frock These frocks they wear, so simply thin,
and pants, as though they believed they walked as men do!

These are indecent and incitements to lewdness in others
by example. *Let me hear more, it is like the strongest*

drink, and I cannot stop And all their talk of soberness,
and farming, and industry, and holiness, and their Living Waters

cannot obscure for us what lies beneath it. A pit that is endless
in darkness, a deep deep pit we must not near the edge of.

The Tree Of Life Tapestry:
Jessie Kinsley, 1927

These braided silks: pale orange, cerise, cerulean blue,
I plait in seemly lines and loops and whorls, I make this visual
music, plump and round and sleek to the fingers. This tree will hold
us up if we let the streams of waters flow down to its roots.

It holds the owl and the squirrel, the peacock and the wren,
the ferret and the lynx, and the Panther of Death itself sits
in its branches. In The Tree of Life we have become its leaves.
The leaves pass through the tree. Around each leaf

is a solid loop of light: it stays in place. We sit
in its branches like birds, and pluck the globed cherries.
The Tree fills the wall of our parlor: when we talk in the evening
after Children's Hour, our eyes move to the rising branches

overhead, and what our children need takes shape there.
We refer to the light and the leaves when arguments arise.
It has taken me many years, and the hands of the other women,
the hands of the children, and the men. It is not my design,

but one I found. It has passed through me, and Father Noyes
and Harriet, through acts of hoeing and cultivation, through
the making of bread, through the cups of milk and the breast
milk given to all the children: each time we look at the braids

it passes through us again. While I was working
I remembered we had fallen from this Tree time after time
inside this house, and entering the world.
I climbed the limbs, straining, over and over, fell

out of the sky of it, breaking. This memory is a shame
I clear away with every silken thread I add here;
the stitches are small and delicate and every one builds up
the Tree of Life we long to live in.   And it is possible,

not a dream but a tapestry of sweet scents: lavender, sage,
rosemary in the kitchen gardens; the cotton and wool
we sew for each other; the faces we have opened,
the open bodies where we suckle the Living Waters,
the stream of leaves we hold in our hands, hold, and let go.

III

Hiding

I have nothing to hide except my soul
and body, and maybe my family history.
I have nothing, I hide nothing, but
nothing is apparent nor disclosed.
I speak the secret, and it remains a secret,
even darker and deeper than before.
I sit for hours staring at the morning
glories, – they are so audacious,
and also the tufted grass and the windows
of another house where people pass
back and forth and bide their time,
preparing to go out into the world
and take their licks, like I do,
only better, for many of them will
concentrate on what's at hand, the
getting and spending and adjusting
and so on, and more power to them
I say and mean it. But I can't do it.
I'm incapacitated for it, I despise it
in a way, but in another way, not.
I'm stunned, perpetually, and all
the fire I've felt has burned
holes in my head. The wind blows
through, and all of my forgettings
are rememberings seen another way.

Filthy Weather

All day the sky darkened and lightened,
darkened and lightened, while it made
up its mind to rain, coaxing itself
into its next phase. And the single
mauve hollyhock glared out of the dark

green, and the ox-eyed daisies flared.
Who minded that the weather was filthy,
that the potatoes rotted in their bin,
that the hummingbird like an attack-
dog dived in on the one already

at the feeder? I didn't mind; in fact
I loved it that things were going badly.
But of course, not really. I wasn't
maintaining the larder, I hadn't cleaned
the floors, the brackish sink. Soft

matter mixed with dark matter and
foul matter. The water drip at
the spigot, rot and violence
the order of the day. My invalid father
fouling the sheets. Senile and anguished,

he tears off his clothes and rages.
I try and try to turn my face
away. The grass here is tall,

thick and weedy, the garden overgrown
and full of ripe tomatoes, and riotous

with rank marigolds and calendula. I have
not plucked a single ragweed, nor gathered
the fruits of the harvest. Rain.
Please rain.

Three Three Three

If you don't go running onward
where will you go?

When you grow old
your brain may crack

and then where will you be?
Nowhere, dispersed beyond belief

and beyond relief of heart.
No ease, that's where.

I've seen it, and I've
heard it every day,

my stroke-tossed father's
broken brain, its wires

sprung out of every sprocket,
repeating "three three three,"

an unhinged number
that he'll never reconnect,

repeating then "nobody, nobody,
nobody," in a lost mournful

tone, the sweetest, precious
nouns gone forever. The bowl

of his head is broken.
The contents, all his nouns

and verbs, have dripped away.
The mercury-drops roll down

below his raw heart's voice,
and that is what we hear.

Immanent

The cool cement floor.
The night gone feral.

The mind and shoulders not
sleeping completely, not

wearing a thin nightgown
completely. Narrow bed

like a launching platform,
a door slamming with a

metallic click. Dream of
a cup not finished, a cool

grotto not entered. A waterfall,
a narrow opening. Voice not

finishing a word. The bed like
a great pod. The legs trembling

beneath the sheet of water,
skewered to the bedsprings

by the shrike. The tan
overcoat of radiant spinal

pain, the rocking motion.
A raven calling from a pillar

of stone, a hummingbird
in the pine tree looking for

nectar. Clutching a blue pillow.
No covering is left. Unsheathed.

Culotte of damaged nerves,
odor of vetiver. The sheen

of the skin. Not finished, not
entered, not opening, not

launched.   Stalled, scintillating.
Not sleeping.

Covering Up

When I saw that I would have breasts
and that they wanted me to cover them up,
I took my shirt off and tied it around my waist
and stomped out into the yard.

I was so furious that no one stopped me;
not my mother, who thought I was acting crazy,
not my father, out working in the hayfield,
not my brother, who thought it was a game,

not my sister, who thought I was acting-out,
who thought I was crazy. I *was* crazy.
For three days I stalked around and stomped,
refusing to wear a shirt. They all said

"Cover up" and to cover up made me feel weak.
I *wasn't* weak: I was damned if I'd pretend,
I was damned. They were two badges on my chest,
each of them saying "This is me."

First the nipples plumped up and turned
from pale pink to dusky rose.
They were two eyes seeing things
my other eyes couldn't see.

Then they rounded out, and ached.
They wondered what was going on,
getting ready for the long story;
nursing mouths, kisses, suckles.

Later, I would stand in the bathroom
with my arms raised painfully
while my husband wrapped a wet towel
tightly around them to bring down the swelling

of too much milk. Later, I would stand
at the lingerie counter and choose a black
lace bra. Later, I would change back
to white cotton. Later, I would burn them.

But that week when I was eleven
I wanted it to be solved, I wanted it to be over.
I took a hoe from the shed and stood bare breasted
outside and beat the hoe to splinters

on the trunk of the maple. I knew it wasn't over,
but I was exhausted. I would have to enjoy
not covering up in secret. That's when
I began to speak in my head as the naked one,

and the other went clothed into the world.

Low Red Moon

Full of watery blood, the soiled skin
of white snow washed pink, and the
stark – there is no other word –
black branches. From the low moan,
wordless, without the grace
of thought, without the consolation
speech could give him, from the
cranked-up bed and the twisted sheet
he cannot draw over his breast
to cover him, from the insistent
daily room, the voice of the nurse
he no longer cares for, from the
montage of dream-scraps – the early
deaths of his brothers coughing blood
 in 1918, spitting in a bowl; the team
of horses, Bess and Clancy; the woman
on horseback who dropped her baby
in the river – from these he cries
to escape. There is no turning
as always in his days before,
no starting over with determined face,
only the long slide, excruciated
every second that he breathes,
and no one – he cries this –
no one can hear his garbled voice
as words received, as words
that lift the weight.

Full Moon: Sitting Up Late
At My Father's Bedside

What can I say. The moon looms in the nighttime sky
with brilliance, as it does. But we are going to touch it,

and then it will go away. The animals on earth
are breathing, but someone takes their hearts

and puts them into broken human bodies.
What can I say to those people? You took the heart

of a chimp: you found you could do it,
and you did? Secrets come out of the heart,

and nowhere else. We don't know how.
What can I say when my father is dying,

with his new eyes and his new heart.
His mind is like a flapping line of laundry,

clothing full of wind. How can I speak
about the babble of his speech? His saying

does not go from here to there, it's only here.
Out of the dog came five pups, slick wet packets,

each different. They grew at different rates.
Some slept, two leapt around all day.

What can I say about their secret selves,
their paws, their separate ways of walking?

What can be said about their natures, and
their flawed and perfect lives? I gave

them away. They have a new trajectory and
I'm still here. I think about them every day.

My father's manner is the same as it was
when he was sane. Senility's a secret, too.

It isn't vague to him. I see intensity in all
he misconstrues, – I think he misconstrues.

The night is brilliant, and the moon's too close.
It calls him out: to where, I cannot say.

IV

Monkey Heart

The monkey mind climbs up a peepul tree
in Bhubaneshwar. Monkey mind, monkey heart,
monkey glands that Yeats paid thousands for
to jump-start his sagging libido. Admonishing
ourselves, we say we're like the chimps, baboons,
and monkeys. But we should be so lucky
as to have such instincts and savanna-smarts,
to survive and thrive without a hat or dress
or shoes. The species we look down on
are not looking up to us. Blue-assed baboons
don't give a rat's ass what we think of
beauty, and I don't think resort to using
us as metaphors or formulating theories
that they sprang from man. They sprang,
and are springing even as we speak, and
if I told you we've been treating them like
dogs you might see what I mean. You'd
say you weren't serious, that some of your
best friends are dogs, and it was just a joke.
A woman in Charlottesville told me a joke
about West Virginians, involving mobile
homes and incest. When I didn't laugh she said
she'd meant no harm, that some of her best
friends were hillbillies. I didn't tell her
to stop monkeying around or that she
reminded me of an ocelot, albeit one
who had gone to Sweetbriar.

And now my monkey muscles
hurt, my monkey throat is dry. I'm
leaping headlong into monkey rage.
Forgive my monkey heart.

Home

This old land pit, green hole,
is filled up with the bones
of all I loved.

The green pit spreads
its foliate of mountain ash,
the sycamores furling and unfurling.

The land is dead on its feet
and this is not the time to visit.
Where I once walked,

green funnel though which
I part the clogged grass,
ragweed and greenbrier.

When I came here first,
it opened greenly.
Where I touched,

it flourished. Now home,
I slog the meadows full
of uncut burnished hay,

its tassels dusting me
with dying pollen.
To retreat to the country

you must have something
to retreat from, fleeing
the beloved, to the beloved.

———

The question here is not asked,
the green wood folds and unfolds
its lapping leaves, and wants

me to become it. I am not becoming
here, but being in the country.
Its wordless haze

soaks into all my days of working
to slim my tongue, darting out
of the twining greenbrier,

digging to clear the fencerows.
This country neither closes nor
uncloses, deep in its austere winter

nor in its leaping summer.
It permitted my feet passing over
for years, my hands unclenching

its catbrier, sharp claws
besides the round-faced daisies.
Each trip back I brought

a luggage stuffed with notes,
a stack of books, a longing,
when I stopped loving the way

the world was combing its hair,
the color of its eyes,
the way it grew its leaves.

This is not the mountain mother,
the hills with green arms.
We give the mountains our names

and they stand still: The Cheat,
The Black, The Backbone.
Because we cared to name them,

we can talk. We make a roughened
music, rubbing up against them,
deep into the grain of sandstone,

the layers of trilobites.
Our music comes out like
a sweet molasses, dark liquid

globing from a fiddle,
falling in dollops from the banjo.
Repeats the ground of repetition,

foliage of burning sweetness.
Deep in Shady Grove the buds unfold
and glow. *Dance Little Fawn.*

The Shelvin Rock. And in the cities
there is another burning
and they want to come home.

⁓

The Tourist Board sings out
the slogan made to pull them in;
Come On Home to West Virginia.

Home; – finally, home.
Here in the woods the grey fox
comes to my doorstep at night

and mangles the cat. *You Left Me
To Die Like a Fox on the Run.*
Every evening the deer emerge

from the dark at the edge
of the trees, flashing their
globed eyes. *Dance Little Fawn.*

The raccoon climbs the ash
outside my window and speaks
a run of clicks and burrs.

To all of them, this house
is a big, odd-smelling tree,
and I, a tall, strange-scented animal.

On the other side of Laurel Mountain
a mine pit looms, and the animals
cross it as they can.

Dark As a Dungeon, Damp as the Dew.
Salt of the earth, burning, caustic.
Down in the hollow an owl cries out

and a plane passes over.
A possum slinks its ancient body
through the leaves, its form

unchanged since the land's upheaval
began. *Possum Up a Simmon Tree.*
Foliate, unfoliate. Bud, unbud.

The roads are looping and winding
through the Appalachians in
switchbacks, plunges, broken pavement.

You Got Your Dead Skunk in the Middle
Of the Road. You got your slaughter.
You got your songs, and your Mack trucks

and your foxes and bears, and they don't care.
You got your rivers: The Gauley, The New,
The Greenbrier, the Gandy and the Sinks of Gandy.

You got your dealers in quilts
and your dealers in coal.
You got your people trying to work

and your people trying to eat,
and they don't care. Come on Home.
Dance, if you can, Little Fawn.

Stained

I'm stained with the iron-red water from the mines
and I'm stained with tobacco and red wine and
the rust of perpetual loss. Near Mabie,
West Virginia I pulled off the narrow road one
morning on my way to work as a substitute teacher.
I wanted to stand there awhile to see how bad
it was, my shuddering in ten-degree weather
on my way to something that couldn't
possibly matter. I had quit smoking and I felt
like a squirrel about to be shot, looking around
in a frenzy. There was a squirrel there, not
afraid at all, turning a hickory nut in its
hands and ignoring me. I must've looked
like what I was, a woman who had lost her
bearings and refused to admit it. It was
another day in my history of posthumous
days, another day when nobody touched my body.

Atavistic

I wanted to walk without clothing
in the woods beside the creek,
and to come to the barn at night

and sleep beside the horses, curled
in the smell and scratch of hay
with the bitch and pups.

The life of the house was flat,
filled with monotonous talking,
passing to and fro among the rooms,

and for what. My mother hated
animals, the way they ate the
food and dirtied the floor.

They were her enemies; she fought
their right to be there and
would have wiped them off the earth

if she could have. If a cat or a dog
came too close to the back door she
threw scalding water on it, and

was righteous in her anger, shouting
that they were not human and
didn't feel real pain.

If we must choose sides, I said
as a child, I take
the side of the animals.

Woods Burning

"The arsonist returned to aid the firefighters."

News story

In the fall of the year
when leaves burn red against
the eye and heart, I go
out hunting for squirrel
and feel the fire of the woods
in my bones. Five thirty
in the morning, cool dry air,
the sun not lighting the leaves yet
and I have left the house,
the coffee and bread, and Molly
slumped on the pillows
like a fallen deer.
Them old quilts smell like the dead,
like my Daddy before me.
Up here, all sweet red maple
and oak in the early time,
gold sycamore and birch.

And when I light the match
for my pipe, I kneel
and light the leaves. They want
to burn, to fill the valley
with a cloud of smoke, the smell
of the meathouse where we hung
the hams and kept the cider press.
Fifty years of smokey air

in the cellar house, my Daddy
before me butchering a shoat
in the fall, the fires
beneath the scalding trough.

And the years of logging,
slash-piles burning and we were
moving on, up the mountain
so steep we held on with our hands,
and from the top we shot the oak log
down the hollow like a giant arrow,
heading for the Kanawha where
the bigwigs sat in the city of Charleston.

I shot my limit of squirrel
and stuffed the bloody things
inside my hunting coat, smell of
blood like iron smelting.
Old Molly should be up by now
watching her programs
in the heated kitchen.
Her Mommy was a tough old bird,
but she wasn't dilatary.
Molly's dilatary, not worth
a hill of beans.

I can smell the good smoke
building up now like
sweet applewood under
the applebutter kettle,
like smoking ham,
the big hearth at the homeplace
where my Daddy tended the fires
every winter morning.

If the wind shifts big now
it will move on down the hollow
to my shack. The years in the mines
he used to yell "Fire in the hole!"
and blow the land to Kingdom Come,
while the trains rolled in
from Pittsburgh. Like my Daddy
before me I can make things happen.
When the fire trucks come screaming
up the river I'll be there
with the rest of them, fighting
the flames, not afraid
to put my hands in the fire.

Redemption

What do you love? Cigarettes, their raw entry.
What do you crave? An easeful death.
In the small blue bedroom with a narrow
hospital bed my father chokes, gags, screams.
What do you need? A better life, one filled
with sweet sadness like a constant feeding
of cream-filled chocolates. What, what?
For God's sake, what is it? Are you going
out in a burning spasm of desire?

My father groans, an incoherent unbearable
sound. His terror-filled old face. The stroke
of a massive hammer. He gargles, babbles.
He hates us, the living; we can still speak.
He chews and sucks his hand; he thinks
it's a breast. Then the flash of a cardinal
outside the window, where he sometimes
stares. What did he crave? His penis
swelled and pained him. Then he died.

I am fused to his damaged body,
his long yellowed history of ninety-six years,
the injuries he gave and took. Reticent and
proud beyond belief, we are. He was.
He twisted and fell, he flailed and cursed.
And then he died, with all the marks
of unsatisfied living all over him. The stroke
of a massive hammer, the yellowed history.

Dark Rain

A morning of dark rain: four wild turkeys walk
stiff-legged at the edge of the leafless woods,
picking at the wet ground. This is early,

before bitter coffee starts to flood my veins,
sluicing into the flesh of my arms and belly.
This is before bitterness tries to take the day,

before my mother falls apart, shouting
"I don't know what to do," before my
grown children precisely point out

my failings. And before all that,
I sat in the one-room school in the country
and identified myself as an eight-year old,

shameful and amazed at what I was
doing there, wearing a faded cotton dress
with gray and purple roses on it,

and hand-me-down brown shoes.
I was about to be given a double promotion
because I could read what they gave me,

although I didn't know who Pearl Buck
might be, or why the Chinese woman squatted
in the field to give birth, or what this had

to do with me. Don't take me literally,
I learned to say in high school, and kept
saying it all along. Sometimes they wouldn't

take me at all: I suppose it was
too much trouble. For awhile,
I saw what death showed me

and said what it told me to say.
It had to happen: I couldn't stop it.
Everywhere I looked, a hand had

 carved a sharp stony outline
around a tree, a flower, the living
blossoms traced in hard lines, the

intricate cold shapes like the screens of
the Taj Mahal, love turned to marble.
For awhile, everything was sharp and cold,

barbed against touch. Death had soaked into
the landscape, dried and hardened it
with dark blood. It had finally taught

me a lesson: I couldn't go on like
I was. I couldn't go on thinking
I was the only one, that the others

were here for my presence. And
my mind reeled and fell on its knees,
my mind I had been so proud of.

Homage To Roy Orbison

If I can touch the voice of Roy Orbison
singing "only in dreams" and if I can

swallow the sweet pudding of his song
then why shouldn't a piece of music

fill in for human contact? Maybe it does
for a second or two, but life is long, or we are,

in our minds, and the singing we do gives us
a taste and not a meal. And what would

happen without it? Would we reconcile
since there would be no contrast, no lift of

Roy's dulcet tones to guide us up to immense
heights of one-pointed ecstasy? So why not sing

as hard and deep as we can? Why not feel out
the song-nerve and trace its trajectory?

I think that in the voice's rise
and wail we finally wake and hear the voice

of an angel. "Sweet dreams baby" Roy throbs.
If so, we go past abrasions and promontories

of broken stony sounds, and emerge up here
where the guitar is a guru, and where Roy's

sweetness is the rule and his sense of form
shapes up this shard-filled life. "Move on

down the line." So there, do it, dance in
a strange way and who cares. When the

listeners judge by their sweetness gauge
and their sucked-in breath at "crying over

you," will anyone care that he dyed his
black hair and had false teeth? I thrash

and shout like a teenage girl for the duration
of the song. "I got a woman mean as she

can be." (I think that's me.) He told me
that anything I wanted he would
give it to me, and you know? He did.

V

Homage to
Baroness Elsa Von Freytag Loringhoven

To hang teaballs from your ears and a caged canary
inside your cloak over your pubis is to inscribe on the outside air
your lobes and singing, and to paste pink postage stamps

on your cheeks is to say kiss me quick on my beauty-mark
and lick my sticky skin. To wear a tomato-can bra tied
with rope around your bust asks the question: What did

you have for breakfast? Who served it up, and why?
Andy Warhol isn't born yet, not by a long shot.
But like Andy, you were snotty and mad. When

a painter whined that she did everything she did
for humanity, you barked "Humanity? I wouldn't
lift a leg for humanity." "You can't touch the hem

of my red oilskin slicker," which you then lifted to
show your butt, fitted with a tail-light. And who
would hold your hand? That slim hand painted

vermilion? When all of Dada thrived, you panted after,
and the dirty little dogs were your only companions
at night in your cold one-room walk-up. And since

the indigent Baron ran away to war, there was no one
to love you. We will hold your hand now that
you're dead, dear Baroness, now that it costs nothing

to laugh at your wacky life. Reading the accounts,
I saw a tall slender woman with an attitude, imperious
in her desires. William Carlos Williams gave her peaches

and money, but later punched her in the face, just
because he wanted her. He said he was "crazy
about the woman." Why do we think our great poets

are enlightened? And I saw the weary face of
the Baroness on her passport photo, after all the
pursuits and rejections, after Duchamp says no

but wants her collaborations, after Williams acts the fool,
after the art scene says Who Cares. Drawn, bruised,
drawn and quartered, giving up, leaving the country.

She knew all about us, wanting to be bold and brave
and beleagured. She knew what she knew and she wouldn't lie,
not even for love. She was nothing but dare, nothing but challenge

and display. Man Ray shaved off her pubic hair and
filmed the act. And after? Nothing. And what did she expect?
Well, what we all expect: a little affection, a little sex, some

help with the bills. But she didn't want a little of anything,
she wanted a lot, and believed she deserved it, and so was
puzzled all her life, her later wretched life. Baroness Elsa,

dirt-poor in Paris, someone left the gas on, and you
never woke, but that is not the end. I adore your Tam O'Shanter
with the silver spoons around the rim, your regal bearing

and your leather aviator's hat. This is not over, because
when I look sideways in the mirror, I see your gleeful,
madeup face. It's only a trick of the light, but

we collect our objects of drama and display,
and icons hate the dark. I set mine out on shelves,
and tomorrow I could appear in a coal-scuttle hat,
pasted with postage stamps, mailing myself to the world.

The Dream Feast

At life's feast someone made me a piña colada
and at the reunion I saw so many relatives
I couldn't recall all their names.
During the feast a car exploded in the parking lot

and injured my cousin Jill who curled up on the cement
and said peacefully she was dying, although she was able
to rejoin us later, pale but recovering after
they washed off the blood. My head was bloodied

too, but I couldn't find time to patch the wound.
A young man in the kitchen found it appealing
and told me I shouldn't bother because the entrance
of a wounded woman in the dining hall would be sure

to attract the attention of men if that's what
I wanted. I wasn't sure that it was.
And then at this remark my brother rose in fury
believing I had been insulted, and offered to fight

for my honor. But just at that moment my sister
Jane noticed her baby daughter was missing and
the rest of the children were looking for her
in the kitchen and under the feasting tables.

She was found at last where a large green
salad had fallen and covered her,
but later was lost again. The children gamely
trooped off to renew the search, calling and laughing.

The entertainment at the feast was wildly varied;
some skits on the little stage, some passionately-
acted plays. My relatives who took part and
wanted so much to get it right stopped midway

to rehearse a scene again and again, and argued
acting techniques. I made a few appearances
but nobody noticed. At the feast it was hard
to fill my plate and find a place at the table

with the blood dripping from my forehead
and the influx of new guests, and the children
everywhere. There were so many we couldn't look
after them and their tripping underfoot prevented

the adults from fully enjoying their meal.
I hadn't had much at all before it was time to go
and I had to gather the children and my aged parents
and two old lovers who wanted a ride. There wasn't

room in the car. The feast had made me ill, but
I waved and smiled and said I hoped we'd do it again.

Adobe

I had no city of my own. That's why I came
here for a season to live beside the huge cemetary
off I 25 in Albuquerque, a city of big clean
sunshine prevailing over eighteen bank robberies
per month and the rage-filled drivers whipping
back and forth through the lanes and redlights
on Route 66, Central Avenue. Driving home
each day I pass a park with a twelve-foot statue
of a flamenco dancer in red skirts, the Gaslite Inn,
the 66 Diner, and the Crystal Dove, and then as
I near the Mount Calvary Cemetary, three blocks
of eroded dirt yards, chained dogs, and ancient
red Fords sinking into their tires. I may as well
have stayed in Appalachia, except for the flesh-
colored adobe houses like little rosy boxes.
Even in the meanest yards, they pulsate and
glow, and serve their purpose like the small
wooden houses at home. There are three colors
here: flesh-and-clay, tan sand, and red. In one
of the red trucks, a man was shot and killed
yesterday by his brother-in-law. Maybe this
single block was the world to them. I think
it was—I know it is to me. As I drive past,
I see how much like human flesh these houses are,
compact and bathed in the orange and
bloodred light of the sunset, hunched
under a huge domed sky.

Handholds

The gold wooden chair sitting by itself
Waiting for you to feel sane

The brother growing bald and borrowing money
The cry of a rabid fox at night

The return to makeup and perfume, even after
There are no more pheremones

The rubbing of the flesh in daylight
The lifted nipples

The broccoli and tomatoes rotting
In the refrigerator

Wild roses burning on the wind
My brother's letters from Korea

The pleasure of cursing someone
You don't know

The little dog who asks no questions
The deliberate, vicious lie

My father bellowing like a black bull
My mother saying it doesn't matter

The college dorm room and the shotgun blast
The red fox snarling in the daylight

The green chair on the porch
The eyes glowing at the edge of the woods

The thrill of the rapid fire
The rabid fox splayed on the grass

The possum with its guts smashed flat
Still lifting its head

The cold click of metal on metal
The satisfaction of the bolt in place

Is this the only handhold we can reach
In the daylight, in the dog's pain

In the wild careening down the turns
Of the road in the rain

Is this it, and it and it   In the drunken crash
At midnight at the edge of the woods

Is this it always for the soldiers and the cattle
For the deer with an arrow hanging from the neck

Is this it forever in the tendons hanging out
In the rot oozing from the wound

My neck, bound and wattled and gasping
My lips feeding the moon

Our answers that maim, our dreams of clutching
Revenge, the bolt and the shot

The yellow chair and the candle waiting
The light and the bright green wall

Face

If you can continue to consider yourself beautiful
although you never were, and your skin continues

to feel like cool velvet, like moist cantaloupe
in the morning, spread with creamy white yogurt,

and if the heart pumps on, and gives itself pause
in the right places, and the train hurries by and you

are happy to see it go and wave your handkerchief,
blinking with satisfaction in the departing breeze, and if all

kinds of leaves continue to fascinate you, the serrated,
the oblate, the thirty shades of green, that lighter

yellowish green the best, the locust with its oddly
tropical look, the Maiden's Bower draped over its arm,

and the holy and imposing oaks that make a grove
for you to enter with gratitude, the grove which appears

in dreams as the innermost place of solace,
and your face has become a repository of thousands

of smoothed-out thoughts and blended miseries, and
these have melded and rearranged everything therein,

then mirrors have become the sites of meditation and
their frames ornate with patterned, copper leaves that help

to remind you of real ones, and your kitchen routines
involve the washing of cups, the drinking of coffee, and

the sweeping and humming, and your face is guiding
you around the room and out to the paths of the garden.

Your face like the philosopher's lamp held up before
the mind, looking and yearning forward with each step,

uncovered and soaking up the rain, peering into
the darkness, where a scarlet hollyhock leans out

to touch it, while the rain sluices down it – no,
it's not like tears – and your face is no longer what it was.

Illuminated Manuscript

Clumped snow, and the faint shafts of afternoon
pierce through the vague windows streaked with grit,

the white room appearing to wake up in spots
as it opens to the meager bolts of sun – as if willing

to be touched anywhere, even in fragmented, instant
gleamings. Light divides and foregrounds the floorboards,

shines on the leaning lighthouse of ruined paper and talky newsprint.
Shapes of broad plant leaves claw forward from their shelving.

Older, distantly brooding, Elizabeth Madox Roberts,
Harriette Arnow, Georgia O'Keefe, look over these stirs

and shiftings from the colored frames I've tried to use
to hold them near me, barely lit by the scanty northern sun.

They are old, gone, or elsewhere in their upright knowing,
fibrillating outward, always, beyond Kentucky and New Mexico,

having their work to do on the other side of the mirror.
Their hair glints white against their chosen backgrounds,

not this room. In lace and denim they admit – while holding
off – selected slants of sunshine. Louise Nevelson in gypsy garb,

boxed in by black and orange, is absorbing her own interior.
To them, my need is like a mote in sunlight, not that they

disown, but own their rooms soaked through with Appalachian
blue, and dense compacted black interiors. The city of

women filled with rooms: vases of red and gold, handworked
stonewear, shot-with-violet glaze, ancient buried urns

of civet oil: passion-flower, sandalwood, the heavy juice of mango,
pomengranate: single white vases of alabaster, tall as the rooms

they inhabit: rooms with hundreds of colored wares
the size of a hand. Vases filled with a load of golden poppies,

slash of red, an iris, baby's breath, tattered camellias,
straw flowers, hawk feathers, quill of chicken, cardinal,

bright need-fire between the rooms, carried back and forth
in a flickering play across our faces. For us,

they are picked out by an occasional beam; for them
the persistence in a single room, working the light

for all it's worth, dark pockets furrowed out by the lamp
at the brow, the Aurora Borealis in a tiny space,

the singular portraits of their choices on their walls.
They can't look back at us, although they made us.

We read their books and memorize their paintings: Watching ourselves
is tiring in our lack of isolate wonder on this side of the wall.

Some pettiness makes us hang too much together, striking our
own interiors. An old woman in workboots is walking from the house

to the barn at midnight, having thought of everything
she's really wanted. A young woman enters a school to talk

with her friends. At night, she gets into bed to sleep alone
even with someone else there. There is a bright flourescence

glowing all the time, a cruel, necessary noise of filaments.
What does it mean to enter the mirror, this tapestry shot with gold,

this illuminated manuscript we need so much we populate it
with our mother's faces, drowning the light in milk,

trying to enter the room of their brooding? Nothing , but to emerge
into these badly lit rooms we each spotlight alone.

At 24

At 24, I had written and read until my eyes were bloodshot,
spending nights and early mornings in a fervor
of page-filling while the baby slept.
I was writing to save my life as I knew it
could be. I was writing to inscribe my body
on a stone tablet, writing in defiance and silence.
Nothing could stop me, I kept saying No
to the paper, I kept saying you can't have me
to the Junior League, to the tiny streets, to impossible
jobs and prissy motherhood. I was certain
there was another way that didn't involve
slavery, another way to love and work than the
simian forms evolved so far. One morning I drank
eight cups of coffee and wrote four poems
and I didn't even care that my head was bursting
and I was lurching around while I scrubbed the bathroom.
Another time I left the children with my mother
and lay in bed all day reading a biography of Van Gogh
and groaning. What a life, what a life.
I thought about Toulouse-Lautrec, that little freak.
I was a freak myself, but only in private.
I stared at his bronzes and terra cottas and oranges
until they pulled the color nerves out of my chest.
That was a long time ago and now I know that
I knew nothing then, and if I had I wouldn't
have gone on. Dear Mr. President, I said, Dear Dean,
Dear Husband, Dear Our Father, Dear Tax Collector,
you don't know me. I don't know what I am,
but whatever it is, you can't have me.

The Walk

Dripping with sweetness, the afternoon spreads
its creamy golden hands over me. What are those
flowers? Jewelweed, some the orange-pink of genital flesh,
some the buttery yellow of soufflé. Then the layer
upon layer of green in the shining afternoon,
the walk that began at the house surrounded by green
grass, then weeds at the side of the path, up through
the layers, the low-growing shrubs, – sassafras,
bayberry with its red knobs in a cluster, sweet gum
with small dry leaves, ferny locust, then the
towering maples and oak, waving and waving, follow me.
Light down through the layers, moving up through
the ladders of rays. God doesn't want anything.

Viridian Days

I was an ordinary woman, and so
I appeared eccentric, collecting gee-gaws
of porcelain and cobalt blue, mincing
deer-meat for the cat. I was unhooked

from matrimony, and so I rose up
like a hot-air balloon, and drifted
down eventually into the countryside,
not shevelled New England nor the

grandeur of the West, but disheveled
West Virginia, where the hills are flung
around like old green handkerchiefs
and the Chessie rumbles along, shaking

the smooth clean skin of the river.
If I wanted to glue magazine pictures
to an entire wall, or walk around nude,
I did so, having no standard to maintain

and no small children to be humiliated
by my defection. I spent years puttering
around in a green bathrobe, smelling of
coffee, perfume, sweat, incense, and

female effluvia. Why not. That was
my motto. I collected books like some
women collect green stamps, but I read
them all, down to the finest print,

the solid cubes of footnotes. Since no one
was there, nobody stopped me. Raspberry vines
slash at the Toyota's sides as I come in.
Flocks of starlings, grosbeaks, mourning doves

lift the air around the house. Fragments
of turkey bones the dog chewed on, a swarm
of ladybugs made into a red enameled necklace,
hulls of black sunflower seeds piled

on the porchboards. Locust, hickory, sweet gum
trees. Absolute silence stricken by crow calls.
Copper pans, eight strands of seed beads,
dolphin earrings. I climb over the fence

at the edge of the woods, back and forth
over it several times a day, gathering ferns,
then digging in the parsley, – shaggy, pungent, green.

Ready

I remember a Sunday with the smell of food drifting
out the door of the cavernous kitchen, and my serious
teenage sister and her girlfriends Jean and Marybelle
standing on the bank above the dirt road in their
white sandals ready to walk to the country church
a mile away, and ready to return to the fried
chicken, green beans and ham, and fresh bread
spread on the table. The sun was bright and
their clean cotton dresses swirled as they turned.
I was a witness to it, and I assure you that it's true.

I remembered this thirty years later as I got
up from the hospital bed, favoring my right side
where something else had been removed.
Pushing a cart that held practically all of my
vital fluids, I made my way down the hall
because I wanted to stand up, for no reason.
I had no future plans, and I would never
found a movement nor understand the
simplest equation; I would never chair the
Department of Importance. Nevertheless,
I was about to embark on a third life, having
used up the first two, as I would this one,
but I shoved the IV with its sugars and tubes
steadily ahead of me, passing a frail man in a hospital
gown pushing his cart from the other direction.
Because I was determined to pull this together,
hooking this lifeline into the next one.

Notes

Page 10: "Clitoral" is based on Thomas Hardy's "During Wind and Rain."

Page 44: "Immanent" owes its form to "Ambush" by Silvia Curbelo.

Page 83: "Handholds" is modeled on Philip Levine's "How Much Can It Hurt?"

Page 88: "Illuminated Manuscript" is patterned after Robert Pinsky's "Faeryland."

Page 92: "The Walk" is dedicated to Maggie Anderson.

Page 95: "Ready" is dedicated to my sister, Eleanor Leary.

Note to The Oneida Poems *Pages 23 to 34*

These poems are based on accounts of and statements by people who were members of the Oneida Community (1847-1881), a community household of around 300 people who tried with intense generosity and thoughtful goodwill to eliminate all selfishness and violence from their lives. They believed that traditional relations between men and women, and especially the institution of marriage, encouraged possessiveness and self-centeredness. Instead, they practiced "Complex Marriage," where each was married to all. Couples came together briefly or for longer periods, and parted by mutual consent. All men in the community were trained to withhold ejaculation, and so there were no unplanned pregnancies. This freed women to take part in all work and activities. Young men were sexually initiated by older women past menopause, and young women by older men trained in "Continence." Besides being practical, it was supposed that these exchanges encouraged "Ascending Fellowship," in which spiritual understanding was conveyed.

The founder, John H. Noyes, called this life Christian Perfectionism, because he rejected the notion of a cycle of sin and forgiveness, and based the community on the belief that the abundant life was really possible if everyone shared responsibility, work, thought, spirit, pleasure, and the erotic life.

Mary and George Cragin were two of the first converts in the original Putney group. Catherine Baker joined and moved with them to Oneida Creek, New York. Harriet Worden was a bright, serious woman who edited the community paper, worked in the trap factory, taught in the community school, and bore John Noyes a son. Victor C. Noyes was the child (a twin) of John Noyes and Mary Cragin, born in the original household in Vermont; he died in the Utica Insane Asylum. Jessie Kinsley was the daughter of Catherine Baker, and along with many others, she stayed on in the Oneida Mansion House after the immorality trials in Utica helped bring the breakup of the community.

While the voices in the poems grow from accounts of real people, they do not always conform closely to historical record.